# THE NECTAR DANCER

# THE NECTAR DANCER

DONALD MACE WILLIAMS

Stoney Creek Publishing

A Member of the Texas Book Consortium

Copyright © 2023 by Donald Mace Williams

Paperback: 979-8-9864078-9-0
Ebook: 979-8-9864078-7-6
Library of Congress: 9798986407890

Cover design by Martha Williams Nichols,
aMuse Productions, Fort Collins, Colorado

Author photo by Dagmar Grieder

# CONTENTS

ASKED AND SENT

# BLOOM AND MINERAL

## A MOUNTAIN REVERIE

She did not take the Rockies' name in vain,
my mother. Doing dishes, being baked
by Central Texas' August, she pronounced
the words as if she heard the Cimarron,
just downslope from our tent, coming pell-mell
so as to radiate the chill of snow
it started from. At six, I had been there
and with my older brother romped like dogs
let loose to run. But the cool mystery,
the reverential transport of each sense,
first came clear to me in the retrospect
of that fixed posture and hushed voice—her hands,
holding the pan she had begun to dry,
motionless, too, in their own reverie.

## TEACHING GOD
*For My Daughter*

God, I have asked God knows how many times,
"Let her be cured soon," and the medicine
that has said to the chosen, "Rise and walk"
is a mere hope for all the rest, like her.
It has come to me what the problem is:
you, being out of time, don't understand
my last word, "soon." So you've made no response.
Let's see if I can help you out. Okay:
we here keep track of our earth's revolutions
around our sun. I've counted eighty-nine,
she, just a fraction of one shy of sixty.
Please make her well with that gap still uncounted.
That will be "soon," see what I mean? And so
we two can hike again before I die.
Wup! That last word! I'll try to help. Okay:

## NAPPING CHILD

Her lids are closed, but the slightest noise
will upset their fine counterpoise
and, like a quick cat, let spring through
their waiting-by-the-front-door blue.

## A FULL MOON FOR ELIZABETH
*September 8, 2022*

I walked my grief this evening to the pasture.
The moon, just risen, dim at first behind
A screen of vapor that would not have been
Seen in a moonless sky, climbed regally
Into dry atmosphere, as round as if
The sky were Euclid's blackboard. We were right
To break loose from rank and from o's that sounded
Like sand tarts that burst sugar through the mouth
When primly bitten. But in lacking rank,
We lack a figure who looks on long strife
By training and tradition as if from
A place above our hanging drapes of smog
And still, dear aunt and mother, looks with love.

## TO MIRANDA AT TWELVE

If I've caught you, it's by extrapolating
from what I've noticed about mockingbirds,
which like to pick out for their imitating
wheel squeaks, cicada shrills, and bluejay words
that mean nyaa-nyaa, drop dead, so's your old man,
but then without a break begin their own
high-soaring riff, sweeter by contrast than
it could have been as song sung all alone.

## THIS IN REMEMBRANCE

Something was always on the stove. We talked
until a lid began to dance, and again
when she came back from stirring. As we sat,
the baking, simmering essence of the food
she had left behind lay all around and was not
itself only but also she, or so
it seems to me: the lustrous ham in the oven,
the moist brown cornbread, and the latticed pone
she made in her last cooking days with straplets
of sweet potato interlaced like fingers,
giving off candy heat and orange-peel spice.
I should be ashamed, I suppose, calling her image
up in a cloud of those warm smells. She had
auras not of the kitchen. Mostly, they
gave back, like planets' rings. A cardinal
once, in a dewy rosebush out the window
of the breakfast nook, flame-red, when I was seven,
set all her form alight, and, "Oh, come look,"
she whispered. With electric force, but dark,
quiet, and, as the causes varied, ironic,
sad, gratified, or wellingly empathic,
her being answered a good line, death news,
word that a grandson had all A's: she glowed
like dormant coals to her world's exhalations.
The red could also cool. Something I said,
damned heartless kid, drove her for three days back
into her sore concavities, the pain
drawn gray around her oval face. Always
it was her people: they controlled. When she
was long past talking, long past seeming to hear,
we waved goodbye after a visit, and
her eyes, from her barred bed, lit up with tears.

Still, my enduring image of her has her
sitting with all of us beside the fireplace
as, from the kitchen, warmth that sums her up
floats all around, enters our lungs, our bloodstream.
Food is what wafts her over the wordless years.

## OAK LEAVES

She had a studious-sprightly walk, this wren,
this girl ahead of me, she on the way
to the brick, and so, to her eyes, alien
library, nearly empty that weekend day.

She didn't hear me behind her, and suddenly
she jumped, as nimble as a browsing doe,
and grasped a sheaf of leaves on a small tree,
caressing them a bit as she let go.

She did the same at the next tree—an oak
again, I saw—and as she stopped for the light
I drew beside, glanced at her, almost spoke,
but she looked down, surprised, chagrined no doubt,

and, more, an Asian, Taiwanese I guessed,
that campus had so many, most of whom
were wary of strangers in the smiling West.
When the light changed, I walked ahead and home.

There, my computer told me that oaks, yes,
grew in Taiwan. I think not mere impulse
had made her jump for leaves, not mere *jeunesse*:
oak leaves, like home. Like home, so little else.

## ELINOR
*After Frost's "The Impulse"*

Spring cleaning had no charms for her,
The house kind,
But when he asked her out on his,
She declined.

That is to say, she didn't answer,
Didn't speak,
His rumbling words evoking just
Her turned cheek.

It wasn't that she didn't love
The clear water,
Or how the calf, licked by its mother,
Would totter.

But he had walked the woods that day
Far longer
Than promised, as if setting out
To wrong her.

She knew the blow to him in not
Replying:
His worst pain, seeing his own words
Lie dying.

She felt avenged, then, in his exit,
Head shaking,
And the long time before she heard
Him raking.

## THE EGG LADY

Though there's no sign, I remember her doorbell is dead
and because the white door is spongy and unresonant
and the television set in the front of the trailer
is going, I have to pound awhile to rouse her.

When the door opens, she stands there not quite
    nodding.
How's the egg supply today? I ask. She rotates
heavily rightward, a sign for me to open
the screen and follow. Over her shoulder:

You want the red uns? Please (though I call them
    brown).
I bend to the window where the living space fades to
    kitchen
and see her barred Plymouth Rocks down the hill
texturing the fenced ground, pecking and scratching.

Rounding the end of the plastic counter, she pushes
the upper of her two waistless circles free
with an arm, her breath loud in the small space,
and she turns around with effort when I say, I've got
    these.

I hand her two cartons. From the refrigerator
she takes two full ones, each of which she opens
to check, showing a feather stuck here and there
but no cracks. I pay, thank her, start toward the door.

Pretty hot lately, I say. Are your hens
still laying OK? She breathes in and breathes out: Yeah.
It's our usual conversation, changing with seasons.

I open the door. She lets herself down in her chair.

See you next time, I say, but she's already engrossed.
As I close the door behind me I hear a girl
saying in a sprightly collegiate accent,
Let's see, I think I'd like to buy a vowel.

## THE NURSING HOME CAT

*The cat seems to have a knack for predicting when nursing*
*home patients are going to die, by curling up next to them*
*during their final hours. (AP)*

I felt you flump up on my bed, by which
I mean I felt the sheet tug, neither leg
having these years since any sense of touch.
So hello, Felix. I'm a little vague
as to the reason we've just now turned friends,
but, you know, I'm a little vague. I look
all down my white length, past my mottled hands,
and see green eyes amid black, merging arcs.
Ah. It is time. The right time, too, the coming
home of my loves, the rounding out of all
I knew: all lines I thought I was enjambing
end-stopped. Come closer, circly cat, and I'll
pull you where I can look you eye to eye.
Yes. Now I know: that deep glow shows the way.

## RAISING MY MOTHER

See, the lab used the part-gray lock of hair
we found in Dad's things, and she's three, her hands
clasped like the same child's whose sweet photo stands
fading on my bookshelf and has stood there
since she died, old and fully unaware
of me, her, anything. And, see, my plans
have worked well, so this child's eyes, heart, brain,
    glands,
are hers precisely, not just to compare.
Now, say, she's lovely and, say, twenty-two,
and on my arm, the march about to play.
I lean and whisper to her—nothing new
to her but, damn me, never heard back then,
in this bride's old age—"I love you," and say,
puzzling her, "What a heartless kid I've been."

## SHE AND THE PLAINS AND I

As a reporter I made more or less a living,
enough to house and feed the four of us
and move us to a new town every time
we had become just settled in the old.
The plains were always home, though, and we came
back when we could, a year or so each time.
I loved the rashness of the whetted air,
and it was on the plains that she was born,
she who was landscape and soft sky to me,
who laughed at Trollope and hop-hopping robins,
whose voice was dark green wheat in April rain,
who in her last hospiced and morphined months
woke up enough to smile at visitors
like a sweet child whose aunts have brought her
    cookies.

For eighteen months my senses have been raw.
I swell behind the eyes at tunes or words
about old times, or at a primrose calyx,
or at calves frisking on a chilly day.
Why almost cry at those? But then, why laugh
out loud at some tired, unamusing crack
in a dull comic strip? Why rage and curse
over a dropped teaspoon? It is as if
the stucco of my moods had been torn off
by gritty winds that left the sheathing bare.

We sat and kissed in my old Dodge a while,
then I got out, and must have helped her slide
the same way, front seats in those days not having
consoles to make sure lovers stayed apart.
We stood in a farm field, stood on the plains

so as to be not in a car for what
I was about to ask, and for her answer,
but in real air and under stars. The answer
was no surprise to her or me. We knew.
How right our sureness was, for long, long years
of moving to new towns, new jobs because
none, somehow, offered me the schedule of
a grantee, with full time and space to write
whatever came to mind, if anything.
That came when I retired, but all those years
she had not muttered, rolled her eyes, or cried
over the moves she must have come to hate.
She had not hedged the yes of that plains night.
Back to her home and mine we came at last,
back to the plains of our love and betrothal,
of her upbringing and my settling-in.
Plains of her wisdom, landscape of my loss.

## LILACS AND SALT
*For Nell, 1999*

I can imagine her as a first-rate oracle,
Though calm-voiced, but she never could have stood
Cave living. Hers is a wisdom that craves air.
Consult her in the kitchen, where she can watch
A marsh hawk skim the pasture, can trim broccoli
While piecing out the auspices. Outside,
Lilacs grow. The odor weaves in her hair,
Her voice exhales it. Now if she will reach,
Mid-prophecy, for salt, and, talking, shake
That out, you'll have caught the flavors, the
    paired hows
Of her delphic what: the fragrance and the wry,
Unlabored word that puts down cant. You seek
An answer; she gives it over her shoulder. Now
Go pondering bloom and mineral on your way.

## FISH TANK

Inside the psychiatric suite, she blinks.
People are there. They're looking at her. Back
To the wall, she sidles to a seat she thinks
May not be dangerous. She is tall and black,

Has on an orange head kerchief with white spots.
She watches tiny fish in a glass world.
They hover, blue, green, scarlet aquanauts
Whose feathered tails a wet breeze has unfurled,

Then dart behind a man-made reef and out,
Not threatening each other, even the bright
Big yellow one lipped in a harmless pout
Like a balloon's mouth, formed to suck, not bite.

Called in, she sits and says, "Reckon who planned
That bunch of lovely little quiet fish?"
"His name, you mean?" he asks, notebook in hand.
"Yeah. Maybe Mr. God? I wish. I wish."

# ONSTAGE, UNFATHOMED

## THE NECTAR DANCER

*News item: Honeybees can tell their fellows where good*
*blossoms are by dancing in certain ways.*

Home from my mission,
vibrant with sweet spice,
feet pricklily lifting,
I dance *A few small,*
*blue blossoms, very choice.*
The others watch me tell,
turn aside, and each by each
buzz back to the field
of yellow clover, rank and tall.

## SNAIL MORNING

When it finally rains, the snails emerge.
They must have drowsed, shell-sheltered and
    withdrawn,
all these dry months in the flower bed and lawn
until the wet night woke a molluscular urge
to cross the driveway. Partway there already
in those few hours, they creep the damp sublime
with campers on on six-inch roads of slime,
bright oozy routes, at a pace they must think heady.
When I back out, the tires are bound to crush
a dozen, travel homes and all, en route.
No other way; I'm in my kind of rush.
I feel it, though, more than I would have done,
say, fifty years ago: I've looked about
and seen too many finish lines unwon.

## LIGHT LUCK

The early sun makes a halo,
A rim, all round a horse
In the grove behind our house
But hides the body in shadow.

I'm sometimes blessed like this
With light luck. At rare moments
I've witnessed tentacled comets
Swimming across the east,

Low moons still moist and great
With earth touch, sun dog pairs,
And sparks from my bride's hair
When she brushed it in the night.

## SUNDOWN YUCCAS

The gentle slope
across the pasture
is white-flecked like a fawn,
each yucca shadow protecting
a remnant heap of the snow
that yesterday lay sock-top deep,
saving the seep of vital
wet for the next day
the way a child lays aside
an all-day sucker at bedtime
to finish tomorrow. In the
morning the sun will take
its half of what's left,
the ground its.
In my thin shadow
past years lie heaped
for if tomorrow comes.

## SILENCE

Dying is like
taking out
your hearing aid.
The clock
stops ticking

## A HORSE IN COVID TIME

I see more people every day
With little feed bags on.
How long, if such a fad holds sway,
Till all the oats are gone?

## THE RAIDS

At last one evening, from his lair
in the foul lake, he could not bear
the sounds of pleasure anymore
from our plank mead hall, just inshore.
He was, himself, as we are told,
a joyless creature, cursed of old
by God's own word. He knew the way
to vengeance. In an unseen spray,
a billion trillionth of his spite
in each vile drop, no door too tight,
he seeped into each dormant lung,
each throat from which glad song had sprung.
The same the next night, and the next.
Soon now some scop's yet unmade text
will tell the rest, how many died
how many times, how many tried
to end the terror, what was done
by what young hero, or by none.

## THE UPPERCASE SCHWA

If I go to bed tired enough, sometimes sleep
oozes around the half-circuit of my pleura
like a small dark *uh* among white ribs.
Sometimes not, and then I try to bring it,
to think that schwa into my chest, like death.
If nothing else, the effort is good practice
for that. I train myself for the big ooze,
the darkest dusk, the schwa in uppercase.
Will it slip unaccented through my chest
or grate as if schwas hated to bear stress?

## THE HAND STENCILS

On the cave wall
A thought survives:
From them to us,
High fives.

**SIX WAYS OF LOOKING AT AN INVISIBLE MAN**

*Researchers are "developing the exotic materials needed to
build a cloak ... intended to steer light and other forms of
electromagnetic radiation around an object, rendering it ...
invisible." (AP)*

1. When he steps into a room, only the blind girl knows.
(The dog thumps its tail on the floor.)
He breathes through his mouth for silence,
he doesn't open a door
with anyone behind it.
He tiptoes.

To him, the advantages of invisibility
outweigh the disadvantages.
Still, he tries to avoid inadvertences,
hoping never, for instance,
to collide with some other observer
also invisible.

2. He acts as if it were something new,
this being seen around or through.
I come from a long invisible line
and all my friends have lines like mine.

3. His speech to a fairly full hall
on what it was like not being seen
drew its loudest applause
from the empty seats.

4. Come in for a drink, she said,
and soon, with a light on low,
they headed for bed.

They undressed, of course, and she,
having gone that far, was game.
But the mystery

for her was thereupon gone
and he, his puzzled frown
unseen, moved on.

5. It started with school, when he was six
and in the fourth grade, reading Proust;
at recess therefore getting whipped.

With a friend he made at MIT
he found the path and was cut loose
from praise, from harm: a glorious day.

6. When he was still new to this style
he went to the mall to stroll awhile,
bought the Times off a coin rack
and held it open, leaning back,
reading and grumbling. Passing there,
a young man blinked: up in the air,
a paper, reading itself aloud.
He backed off, pointing. Soon a crowd
had formed. A woman screamed and fell.
Another. Soon there was a swell,
a backward-surging, foaming wave,
a writhing, many-tonsiled rave.
He laid the paper, folded, down
and went home, having learned at last
how power felt. It was a blast.

## GLITTER

It's too cold out this morning for real flakes.
What come come like sea salt being ground fine.
I know they're there only because the air
is out of focus migrainelike and glinting.
And yet the ground is white an inch or so.
This must have gone on all night, though when I
looked out the door at bedtime, one hand shielding
my eyes against the streetlight, nothing showed.
When it is this cold, our six months of drought
are only reasserted by what falls.
We want moisture to swell motes into flakes
that when they land lie like small melting tents
so we and our poor breathing ground can take
soft air into our lungs again at last.

## CONNECTIONS

An aspen grove is all one tree, a text-
book says, white, columned trunks sprung from a sing-
le root, the sole begetter, the clan chief-
tain, who long since has stood in anonym-
ity among the ranks he thrust through fresh-
charred soil to form, first after fire.
My neighbor,
far from the usual aspen altitudes,
has one, not more, next to his house, a healthy,
small, sturdy tree whose leaves turn gold and shimmer
in prairie wind as if amid a color
ensemble high up in the Rockies. There
there therefore may exist more singles, set
whitely amid spruce groves, their solitary
selves brightening, each, one small autumn scene.

## RAIN QUOTES

Gone these months past,
raindrops drop notes
in small air quotes,
'home, home at last.'

## LAPLAND LONGSPURS

These birds spend springs and summers so far north
we never hear them sing, which is too bad
because they sing in dizzy flight, like larks.
They come here to stay warm, the flocks of snowbirds
that from the road we take for low black clouds.
Then the cloud wheels, shuffles itself like cards,
fans out, does dark sand paintings in the sky
or quick-change fireworks shows in solid black:
a comb; a wheel; a straight-up elegant vase
made of black wings, two thousand pairs, that stands
on some sky mantel we can't see. Birds, birds,
who can say why, hang in close-order drill,
flying in place, sky mimes, from many, one.
And God knows where the order comes from when
a trickle a bird-body wide appears
at the left bottom of some form and all
poofs into one black sweeping line of speed
and wings into the wings. The show is over.
Up the road, though, another flock will be
onstage, unfathomed, doing its precise,
never repeated shapes, a lantern show
projected on the air with birds the shadows.

## KÖCHEL ZERO

Mountains, seen, tumble like a sea
or a Mozart symphony
one of the great last three.

Plains are cut clean-edged into blue
not to view
to live on and be you.

## DRY GRASS, FIRST SNOW

The waiting prairie rust-
les, raw linguine, thrust-
up tongues for Eucharist.
Cool wafers. *Missa est.*

## REMNANT GREEN

Green grass recedes to brown,
its underlying hue.
Drought sucks the greenness down
underground, out of view.

Bad for the calves that graze
beyond the wire, but I
take pleasure at mid May's
art with a brush gone dry.

Brown is the ruling tone.
Still, here and there a streak
of remnant green is shown,
part hope, part good technique.

## ASPENS TURNING

The aspens are turning, my neighbor said.
I went to see. Mostly gold, some red,
They stood and whirled, their white trunks bare.
A bright sheen (spun gold) filled the air.
The whole big hill was turning, too.
Trees from the back came into view.
I tried with a toe and nearly fell,
Like stepping on a carousel.
Here came two close-together trees
Filled up with dizzy chickadees,
And some were upside down and clinging,
Some rightside up, but all were singing
A small, excited dee-dee-dee
As if to say, what a crazy tree.

## BLUEBONNETS

Bluebonnets are my state's official flower.
That must in part be why I've loved them since
My boyhood years amid massed pastures of them,
Which sail-white tops and subtle clay-red freckles
Made bluer yet than all-blue blooms could be.
I learned in school the flowers' formal state,
And learned about the heroes of the Alamo
And San Jacinto, and the humdrum song
The state also adopted as official.
"All hail the mighty state," it says, and rhymes
Of course on "great." Too bad the lyrics didn't
Show some influence of the flower's art,
The clean, blithe white and the reticent red
That deepen, by contrasting with, the blue.
Visitors see the fields as single-shaded.
I'll grant they seem so from a long way off.
I've known the close-up truth too many years,
Starting with shoeless walks when bluebonnets
Came halfway up my shins, to think the blue
Is merely that. Stop and get out, I say,
Some early April and wade in. (Watch, though,
For rattlesnakes.) Bend close, and see, I hope,
The shades of beauty the road view concealed.

## BIG THOMPSON

It comes on down between the meadowy banks
Open and free, so copious a flow
I wonder at the capacity of mountains,
Giving and giving water as if it were air.
They must be practically hollow beneath their rocks,
Their reservoirs resounding to the play
Of snowmelt springing through, the depths like oceans,
To quicken this sweet current so many a year.
Coming from dry country, I shake my head
At all this vital rush, this miracle
Of continuity, not a mere surge
After a rain that then subsides, brief, red
Water into red earth, but forever full,
Its pump the slow flank of the whole Front Range.

## ∞ RANCH

It took forever, driving across West Texas.
Partway there I saw the brand of a ranch,
Infinity, over a cattle guard, up in an arch.
I stopped and rolled down the glass of my Lexus.
Just the right setting for such a concept to rest,
I thought: unlimited space beyond the gate.
(True, the sign also had words: The Lazy 8,
Picked no doubt by some cowboy of infinite jest.)
I saw the brand, too—this seemed a bit absurd—
On the fat hips of an entirely finite herd.

## CANYON TEMPLES

In the red wall has stood for eons
a Petra, carved along their way
by those nomadic Nabataeans
Water and Wind, who never stay.

## RAINBOW TROUT

He hangs amid glass towers and crystal ropes,
the water slipping past his sleekness
then crashing, sunlit, like a burst geode
beyond the studded brink.
His spotted tail and brilliant flanks are all
one muscle, and one undulation
snaps him across the pool to where a twig
pulsing down an uncased pipe of current
shows a gray tip, a head.
Back home, he hovers, mouthing atmosphere,
his vehicle, his Earth, his bringer and giver
the green, chill, intricate, capricious
harmony in which, by which,
as part of which he lives, to which
the quivers of his unity are tuned.

## ON A PIANIST'S EIGHTIETH BIRTHDAY

Some tunes are like a horsefly on the trail
circling close to your ears for miles, unbrushable,
though he's outside and they, buzzing unhushable,
inside. You need a brainwash or a flail,
a trephination, something. How a tune
can take charge like that, God knows. Does God know?
Music must be his, may be him. If so,
why plague us with God humdrum, God jejune?
But now and then the tune that's visited
on you is him, is you, and welcome to
stay, say, a lifetime rounding in your head.
Mozart's C minor, the slow movement's start,
serves. Keeping it, to ride it, guide it through
the horseflies is the main thing, is the art.

## THE COMPOSITOR
*Vienna, 1819*

I'm like those players of the *Musikfreunde*,
only instead of tails I wear an apron.
Or, no, I'm like the man who wrote from left
to right the notes that I drive into pewter
from right to left all the long day like some
great woodpecker, pounding a flat-faced maul
onto this punch or that that I've grabbed up,
not looking, from wood cases that stand bristling
with metal music like the backs of hedgehogs,
repeating in reverse his propped-up pages,
playing them on my kind of *Hammerklavier*.
Why working backwards hasn't turned me cross-eyed,
you tell me; but I've done it forty years,
starting when I was nine, before my father
flopped at the music-printing business, selling
shop, stock, ink, metal, and good name for almost
nothing, but with one firm entailment: keep
this young man in your employ all his life.
He could have got more by not putting that
into the contract. Then I might have kept
learning *Klavier*. If that proved not to make
my fortune as the maestro said it would,
this or some other printer would have jumped
to hire a man who could read notes and staffs
better than words, whose fingers flicked among
the punches for whole note, half note, bass clef,
sharp, flat, rests, treble clef, eighth note, as if
playing glissandos, chords, and trills, his eyes
fixed on the score, bravura strokes stamp-stamping
each sign as clear as if it were his mind
making this work up, not his hands obeying

the manuscript a man his same age wrote.
I rarely hammer home an eighth for a quarter
or sharp a G that should have been a flat,
and yet a proof came back one day with this
scrawled in the margin: You damned fool! I'd like
to see him play the steel keyboard I play,
to punch in ten days what I punch in one,
he who of all composers ought to know
the temper of my life, spending my days
amid a million notes I never hear.

## THE CUTTING HORSE EVENT

Cut out of the herd Lord knows how long ago,
the calf by now seems only half intent
on outmaneuvering the horse. He almost
sags as he feints left with a bent front leg,
then runs, listless, the other way. He's learned
long since he can't outwit this grim athlete,
who mirrors every move he makes. It's like
trying to get around his own reflection.
Closely the dark eyes in the lowered head
watch him, quickly the hulking body moves
between him and the herd he was born into,
the packed half-circle of his kind, protective,
warm, watching with muzzles laid across
their neighbors' backs, glad not to have been cut
out from the herd themselves. And he, at first,
frantic, cast longing glances their way, homeward,
as he dashed left, right, front. Exhausted now,
and as if nearly reconciled to apartness,
he makes his feeble move.
A buzzer sounds.
The horse stands with head up, indifferent.
With joy the calf spurts past. There is the herd,
sought till the seeking had become a dream,
waiting, hides, heads, and hair. Kicking up dust,
he runs across the arena with tail flying,
home at last. In relief he barely notices
how the herd, on his arrival, backs away.

# ASKED AND SENT

## CONSOLATION FOR THE ETERNALLY CURIOUS

When we go
If we know
We'll know
We know.
If we don't know
We won't know
We don't know

## THE RIGHT WORDS

But how will I know what to say
and how will I know how to act
when I am going on my way?

It can't be long until the day,
I'm quite accepting of that fact.
But how will I know what to say?

Should I have phrases tucked away,
bright images all ready-packed
for when I'm going on my way?

Or if that memorized display
would seem too stiff, too cleanly stacked,
then how will I know what to say?

I've never been disposed to pray
aloud. My friends would think me cracked
and overdue to go my way.

One thing: if words do deign to stray
my way, I'll need time to redact,
or I won't know how best to say,
goodbye, I'm going on my way.

## TIME ZONES

When I drove east, the sun hung tall,
distance kept adding to the time.
But westward now the hours get small.

I used to fancy youth was all,
since, once well launched into its climb
as I drove east, the sun hung tall.

I thought a wish would make it stall
straight overhead, poised in its prime,
but westward, now, the hours get small.

As time beneath me moved a-crawl
I found the scenery sublime
when I drove east. The sun hung tall

and though my youth was past recall
I never knew it. What a crime
how, westward now, the hours get small.

My clock, as in a windy hall,
strikes with a disappearing chime.
When I drove east, the sun hung tall
but westward, how the hours get small.

## ZERO EBB

It's as if the wind were switching
from south to north
and the interim, this time,
were one long exiled breath
that never comes home,

and cytoplasm, once rippling
in ten trillion lakes,
at zero ebb, dead calm,
the whispers of every dock's
pilings struck dumb.

# THE TENSES OF MAN

Am.
Will.
Haven't.
Couldn't.

Want to.
Going to.
Tried to.
Didn't.

Now.
Soon.
Not yet.
Not.

## WIND AGAINST

My bones seemed hollow like birds' all through
    my walk
east up the street. I thought it was just health
but then, at the end, I turned homeward and felt
lead in the role of marrow, an instant swap.

Struggling now instead of springing, I bent
into surprising and quite unfair resistance.
When I catch my breath I want to ask some physicist
is wind in favor less than wind against?

## THE VOICE OF THE DOVE

I've loved the mourning dove since I was a child—
the soft, suffusing sound that always calmed
me then as it does now and must calm, too,
all those that hear it: people, grass, the sky.
I think the tone, taken two octaves down,
would sound like Jesus' voice when, at the tomb,
John says, he spoke one word, "Mary," to her
who wrung her hands, not knowing who stood there.

# INCLUSIVENESS, MR. YEATS

His hour come round, he shrugs and is out.
There's the cord to sever,
Then he's slouching blandly about,
The Great Whatever.

## THE FOOT-DRYING

Her hair fell thick and soft across his feet,
caressed them with a hovering womanness,
a proxy of her lips, almost as sweet.
About how he felt then, we have to guess.

Being, Pound said, a man, "no capon priest,"
did he hang nightly from a cross of no,
burn at that foot-drying to be released
for an hour with her, for the elders to rise and go?

He had the power to order things that way,
to draw young women into dim back rooms
regularly. The gospels never say,
no wheres or whens, if so, nor hows nor whoms.

To say so would of course have seemed a breach,
unholy and, besides, impolitic,
not well-designed to help the future teach
a heaven-sent perfection, the mystique

required to draw in multiples of masses,
burgeoning at the word of something more,
reward, reunion, when the present passes.
So if we knock, no one unlocks that door.

It may be just as well. If he in fact
did love and word had sped upslope, downslope
across the earth, the future would have lacked
a godly image. And lacked, therefore, hope.

## FORGETFUL MOUTHS

In the drought, rain prayers from a million farmyards
    must
have gone up, Send, please Send, through gritty jaws,
but the only answer we got was more dust
scratching our faces like gnats with silicon claws.

Now it has rained. The few leftover clouds
this morning have pink undersides, a sky
as soft as words raised by forgetful mouths
that take this as the asked and sent reply.

**AFTER THE SUICIDE**
*May, 1945*

He stands, gone now his sound and Fuehry,
before one Man, both judge and Jewry.

## THE TOLL TRAIL

It is a guilty trail that I am on:
Moss campions beside it thickly flung—
Bright words stamped on green where my eyes have
    gone—
And raspberries, keen music on the tongue.
Alpine firs still, too, tall as I and slimmer,
Young yet, kin to each other and to me
(My boast, not theirs), and, with a woody shimmer,
Heather, pale blooms enlightening dark scree.
Guilty, because why should I be trail-blessed
With words and music, progeny, and her,
When I have no toll ready for the crest
But pocket change my fretful fingers stir?
Lord, help me swell my coinage so you,
Camped at the top, may judge it my trail's due.

## WORDLESSNESS

When I'm outside and a cool breeze springs up,
I think *oh great, delightful.* Then I wonder
how robins, say, or jackrabbits enjoy it
without the words to tell their senses so.
My pleasure, like my pain, has to pass through
the filter of the alphabet, not like,
say, horses, which express their joy by running,
or mockingbirds, which seem to sing more brightly.
But I, spreading my arms to the cool air,
think words for what I feel, so it's removed
one step from real. For real, I need to shed
word power and even keep myself from thinking,
"Good, it's gone now. No words at all. Aphasia."

## DEFENSE

Some great and hungry fish in view,
The squid hides in an inky cloud.
Though my defenses may be few,
This one, I, too, have been allowed.

## UNRECONCILED
*2018*

October leaves: I am unreconciled
to its, and their, departures. Give me more.
Let gold have stayed on trees, not just have whiled,
or let it be fit, fallen, to restore.
I loved leaves fallen when I was a child,
their yellow peltings, pelted yellows piled
on still-green grass. Now I say, please, no more.
This evening, in the full-care home, so styled,
as her and others' wheelchairs crowd the floor,
October leaves. I am unreconciled.
I want this fall to linger, gray and mild,
like those we loved in many a fall of yore.
Leaves leave, falls fall. I am unreconciled.

## CONTRARY TO FACT

If she were here, I say as I drive by her door
(for conditions contrary to fact: the subjunctive: "were"),
I would kiss her for the first time ever at her front step
    once more
and think once again, I'm going to marry her.

In the indicative, for things as they really are,
it was a year and a day ago I kissed her last, last fall,
and the right verb, sounding unstoppably near and far,
keeps saying its name, was, was. Was then. Was all.

## Z TAPPING

I know only this much computerese:
things happen when you finger certain keys
such as Control, held down, and then tapped Zs.
That brings about a word-by-word reprise
of something once gone. Moving finger, please
tap faster, longer, till my tired eye sees
all that were gone come back, realities
again, not wispy thoughts of used-to-bes.

## ESSENCE

Consider the tomato,
fresh from out back,
the sun warm clear down to the seeds
in the juicy flesh.

The essence of tomato,
one of us says,
and I think, tasting, how it selves,
that Hopkins word.

Does it so? A tomato
from the garden is good
because it smacks of all its kind.
Not apple. Not plum.

We quarter another tomato
off the same vine.
The sections glisten red with juice.
I taste, and the tang

is as bright, as much tomato
as the other was.
Still, it's itself, not quite the same
a tomatoness.

I try: can I think tomato
and not think taste?
Were this and that, before we ate them,
each its own,

its way of being tomato
not of the juice,

the peels, the redness, roundness, not
even the seeds,

distilled beyond mere tomato
taste and flesh?
I'm talking of self, now, true essence—
But what's the use?

It's not about tomatoes.
I want to know
if an essence—sans flesh, juice, seed—can kiss
another essence.

## THE QUESTION

We're born head down, knees bent,
like the Spanish mark that says
here comes a question.

Death comes then, holding
his curved blade one-handed
and upright, meaning
the question has ended.

## PEACE EMBODIED

When I step past the last house on my walk
and see the long edge of the plains, with sky
behind, I don't say to my ribs, relax,
be soft. There isn't time, because my eyes
have taken charge and been obeyed. Calm, now,
they said, and instantly I was serene,
a benediction of parental air
down to the very toenails of my lungs.
When I was small and threatened, and in fact
last week, though then it was by circumstance
and not a freckled bully, I remembered
there was such caring air, and then I felt
peace like that be, not come, as if it was
there all the time, waiting for eyes and sky
to make it known in full embodiment.

## CARRYING ON FOR A WRITER

He got anesthetized, that time, and then
he was in bed, looking up at a smiling face,
being asked, how do you like your brand-new knee?
It was exactly like that when he died,
only there wasn't any "and then." So he didn't
see his book covers seem to pulse, as if
life in there was still beating, wanting out.
It's up to us, the thought went book to book
along the shelf. That was what he had asked,
and all that lacked now was a smiling face
above a lifted cover, saying good morning.

# ACKNOWLEDGMENTS

Acknowledgments of previous publications

"This in Remembrance," *Friends Journal*

"Oak Leaves," *National Review*

"The Nursing Home Cat," *descant*

"Elinor," *The Raintown Review*

"The Egg Lady," *Tar River Poetry*

"On a Pianist's Eightieth Birthday," *Atlanta Review*

"Defense," *Bibliophilos*

"Light Luck," *San Pedro River Review*

"The Question," *Spillway* and *Wolfe and Other Poems*

"Raising My Mother" and "Fish Tank," *The Eclectic Muse* and *Wolfe and Other Poems*

"Lapland Longspurs," *Candelabrum*

"The Nectar Dancer," *Mature Years*

"The Foot Drying" and "Wordlessness," *The Road Not Taken*

"The Toll Trail," *Anglican Theological Review*

"Lilacs and Salt," *The Amherst Review* and *Wolfe and Other Poems*

"The Voice of the Dove," *Ancient Paths*

"Essence" and "The Cutting Horse Event," *Langdon Review of the Arts in Texas*

"Snail Morning," *Slant*

"A Horse in Covid Time," *Light* online

"The Hand Stencils," *Wolfe and Other Poems*

"The Compositor," *American Arts Quarterly*

"Inclusiveness, Mr. Yeats," "Dry Grass, First Snow," and "Wind Against," *Chronicles*

"Aspens Turning," *Society of Classical Poets Journal*

"Bluebonnets," *San Antonio Express-News*

"Infinity Ranch," *The Texas Observer*

"Rainbow Trout," *Trail & Timberline*

"Canyon Temples," *Better Than Starbucks*

# ABOUT THE AUTHOR

Donald Mace Williams is a retired newspaper writer and editor with a Ph.D. in Beowulfian prosody. His poems have appeared in three dozen magazines and in the books *Wolfe and Other Poems, Wolfe* and *Being Ninety,* and this one. Williams has also two novels and two nonfiction books, including *The Sparrow and the Hall* and *Interlude in Umbarger.*

Williams is ninety-three years old and continues to write poetry and translations. He lives alone and independently in the Texas Panhandle.

CPSIA information can be obtained
at www.ICGtesting.com
Printed in the USA
BVHW042300230723
667551BV00002B/11